Mother Teresa

Vanora Leigh

Illustrations by Richard Hook

The Bookwright Press
New York · 1986

Great Lives

William Shakespeare
Queen Elizabeth II
Anne Frank
Martin Luther King, Jr.
Helen Keller
Ferdinand Magellan
Mother Teresa
John F. Kennedy

First published in the United States in 1986 by
The Bookwright Press
387 Park Avenue South
New York, NY 10016

First published in 1985 by
Wayland (Publishers) Limited
61 Western Road, Hove
East Sussex BN3 1JD, England

© Copyright 1985 Wayland (Publishers) Ltd

2nd impression 1986

ISBN 0–531–18033–6
Library of Congress Catalog Card Number: 85–72245

Phototypeset by Kalligraphics Ltd, Redhill, Surrey
Printed in Italy by G. Canale & C.S.p.A., Turin

Contents

The little nun

One of the most moving sights to come out of the horrors of shelled and devastated Beirut in 1982 was that of a little, elderly nun, cradling the tiny body of one of the thirty-seven mentally retarded children she had rescued from a bombed hospital. She had only been in Lebanon for twenty-four hours.

1985 had hardly begun and there was this same little nun, now in Ethiopia, where millions were suffering from famine and starvation.

Wherever there is human misery and hunger, that nun, known throughout the world as Mother Teresa of Calcutta, can be found with her followers, doing their best to ease the suffering.

The squalid Calcutta slums where Mother Teresa first began her work.

She once said: "We ourselves feel that what we are doing is just a drop in the ocean. But if that drop was not in the ocean I think that ocean will be less because of that missing drop."

One of Mother Teresa's favorite expressions for describing the work that she and her followers are busily engaged in is, "let's do something beautiful for God." That work may be helping and caring for lepers in India, or venturing into war-torn Lebanon to rescue the children and the handicapped.

Mother Teresa was born in Macedonia, in what is now a part of Yugoslavia. She has worked for the very poorest people in India (and later throughout the world) for almost forty years. Although she is now in her seventies, she continues her work, as tireless as ever.

In 1979, Mother Teresa was awarded the Nobel Peace Prize. No one could have deserved this honor more, for she has lived her whole life according to the words of her own prayers: "Make us worthy, Lord, to serve our fellow men throughout the world who live and die in poverty and hunger."

"A nightmare city"

Calcutta, where Mother Teresa began her work, in 1948, is a huge, sprawling city in northeast India. It is a city of stark contrasts, where rich men's homes overlook some of the worst slums in the world. Calcutta has a population of over five million, and about one million of these people spend their entire lives on the city's streets.

Calcutta was the capital of India from 1833 until 1912. It is situated on the Hooghly River and is an important port and a great industrial center.

The centre of the city is like that of many other large towns. There are parks, stately office buildings and modern apartments and offices. However, the city outskirts are very

different. Here there are huge slum areas of terrible squalor.

Housing in Calcutta is a very big problem, because every day more and more people flock into the city from the villages of India, looking for work and food. Homes for these people are mud huts or hovels made out of gasoline cans and covered with rough burlap or pieces of plastic. These flimsy structures provide little protection from the torrential monsoon rains.

Yet many people haven't even these hovels to call home. Whole families live on the sidewalks or under bridges. Many camp out, night after night, at bus stops or on railroad station platforms. There, they sleep, cook and eat what little food they have been able to obtain from begging or from the city's refuse bins.

Once Calcutta was known as the "City of Palaces," but more recently it has been described as "the City of Dreadful Night" and "a nightmare city."

A happy childhood

A street in present-day Skopje, the town where Mother Teresa was born.

Mother Teresa was born on August 27, 1910, in Skopje, Macedonia (later to become part of Yugoslavia). Her Albanian parents christened their daughter Agnes Gouxha Bejaxhiu. They already had one other daughter, Aga, who was five years old, and a son, Lazar, who was two.

The Bejaxhiu family were devout Roman Catholics and the father, Nikola, a storekeeper, was an Albanian patriot, deeply involved in politics. Arriving home from a political meeting one night, he collapsed and was taken to a local hospital where he died.

Nikola's widow, Dronda, managed to keep the family together by starting a small embroidery business. Despite the loss of their father, Mother Teresa remembers that they were always a very happy family.

Although she attended a non-Catholic government school, the

young Agnes became increasingly interested in religion, particularly in the work of missionaries. She was fascinated by stories of people she knew who had gone to India. At the age of twelve, she amazed a church meeting by pinpointing the exact location and work done by each mission, on a map of the world. At only fifteen, after reading letters sent home from missionaries working in Calcutta, she asked to be sent out to work for the Bengal Mission.

When she reached the age of eighteen, Agnes knew it was time for her to leave her happy home and become a missionary nun, working for the poor. Her brother Lazar, an army officer, was horrified at her decision. But Agnes had no doubts. She was convinced that it was God's wish that she should do this work.

Many years later, she said: ". . . since then, these fifty years, I've never doubted even for a second that I've done the right thing; it was the will of God. It was His choice."

The teacher

Shortly after her eighteenth birthday, Agnes Bejaxhiu left Yugoslavia forever. She was sent first to Rathfarnham Abbey, near Dublin, Ireland, to join a teaching order, the Loreto Sisters. After a few weeks, the young novice was on her way to India, to become a missionary in the beautiful hill town of Darjeeling.

Besides being famous for its tea, Darjeeling was also a center of education and it was at the Loreto convent that Agnes began her work, teaching the daughters of wealthy families. It was here, also, that she took her first vows as a religious Sister and changed her name to Teresa. She chose the name in honor of the French saint, Thérèse of Lisieux, known as the Little Flower of Jesus.

The mountain scenery around Darjeeling may have reminded the young girl of her native Yugoslavia, but she was not to stay there for long. After a short time she was sent to the teeming city of Calcutta.

For twenty years, St Mary's High School, a convent in Calcutta, was home to Sister, later Mother, Teresa. It was run by the Loreto Sisters for Bengali girls, and Mother Teresa taught them history and geography. Eventually, she became headmistress of the school and is still remembered as an energetic and dedicated teacher.

Yet, despite her success, Mother Teresa was uneasy in her pleasant surroundings. The school was set among beautifully-kept lawns and gardens, but on the other side of its wall lay one of the worst slums in the world. From her room in the convent, she was able to see the dreadful squalor, and she was distressed by the knowledge that people had to exist in such terrible conditions.

Older pupils at the convent were encouraged by Mother Teresa to visit the people in the slums, taking food with them. On one occasion, Mother Teresa gave up her bed for the night to a beggar-woman who had come to the convent door.

A mother washes her baby on the Calcutta street which is their home.

While on a train journey, Mother Teresa was inspired to work among the poor.

Inspiration Day

Among Mother Teresa's many followers, September 10 has become known as Inspiration Day. On that date, in 1946, she was on a train when, as she has described, ". . . I heard the call to give up all and follow Him into the slums to serve Him among the poorest of the poor."

But first she had to get permission to leave the Loreto Order and the convent. She told the Archbishop of Calcutta about the work God was calling her to do, but he would not give her permission to go. India, in 1946, was on the verge of independence from Britain, and the Archbishop was afraid that it would not be safe for a European woman to work alone in the slums.

Certain that God's will would be done – eventually – Mother Teresa patiently bided her time. Together with some of her pupils, she took first-aid equipment into the streets and founded a little dispensary for the sick.

Setting off on her own

In 1948, Mother Teresa was given permission to leave the convent. She has said that it was difficult to leave such a peaceful place for the noisy, dirty Calcutta streets.

One of her first actions was to discard her black robe and replace it with a simple white cotton sari, bordered with blue. It cost only four rupees (about 35 cents). Then, knowing that she must have some medical knowledge, she spent several months with a group of medical missionaries in Patna, some 600 kilometers (377 miles) northeast of Calcutta.

Mother Teresa returned with just five rupees but, undaunted, she set up a little school in the middle of the slums. There were no desks or chairs, not even a blackboard, so she wrote the Bengali alphabet in the dust with a stick! On the first day, only five children attended the school, but twenty years later, there were five hundred.

The Missionaries of Charity

In her simple white sari, Mother Teresa soon became a familiar sight in the slums of Calcutta. She shared the slum dwellers' meager existence and diet, often just rice and salt. In addition to running her school, she set out on foot each day, distributing food and medicines.

In 1949, the first of Mother Teresa's followers came to join her: Subhasini Das, who later became Sister Agnes, and Magdalene Gomes, later Sister Gertrude. They had both been pupils at St Mary's High School. Later, they were joined by other former students who gladly gave up their pleasant homes to work with their beloved Mother Teresa in the dirty alleyways that were "home" to so many of Calcutta's poorest citizens.

In 1950, Mother Teresa received the Pope's blessing and his permission to found her own

reward, "wholehearted and free service to the poorest of the poor."

As the number of her Sisters began to grow, Mother Teresa searched for a large house to accommodate them all. At this time, she wrote in her diary, "I thought how much the poor must ache in body and soul looking for home, food and health."

A house was eventually found. The Archbishop of Calcutta advanced the money, and before long, 54a Lower Circular Road, Calcutta, became one of the most famous addresses in the world – the "Mother House" of the Missionaries of Charity.

order, the Congregation of the Missionaries of Charity.

Life for the Missionaries was very hard. Mother Teresa emphasized that, in order to understand the poor, the Missionaries should share the same hardships and deprivations as the people they were serving, by living among them. Like Mother Teresa, they wore simple white saris with a small crucifix on the left shoulder. Besides their vows of poverty, chastity and obedience, the nuns also undertook to give, without

The headquarters of the Missionaries of Charity in Calcutta.

A home for the dying

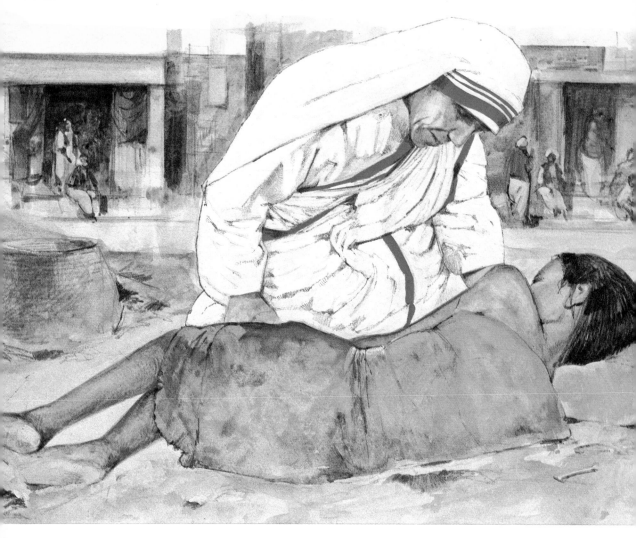

One of the most dramatic events in Mother Teresa's life took place one day in 1952. As she walked past a busy Calcutta hospital, she saw a dying woman lying on the pavement outside. Mother Teresa carried the woman into the hospital, but the staff refused to let her stay – she was too diseased and too poor, they said. An outraged Mother Teresa refused to move until the woman was, at last, given a bed in which to die.

This tragic episode made

Mother Teresa more than ever aware that a home was needed in which destitute and abandoned people could die in peace and with dignity. She knew that there were many more people dying in the gutters of Calcutta every day. So she went to the city council to see if they would provide her with a suitable building.

She was shown two large rooms, once used as a pilgrims' hostel, attached to the temple of Kali, the Hindu goddess of death and destruction. These rooms were then being used by drop-outs, gamblers and drug addicts. Mother Teresa accepted this accommodation, and within a day, her first patients were admitted. Some were brought in on wheelbarrows; one was found dying in a refuse bin.

Mother Teresa's Home for the Destitute Dying was given the name *Nirmal Hriday*, which means the Place of the Pure Heart, although it is sometimes referred to simply as Kalighat, after the name of the temple. Soon there were plenty of girls anxious to help Mother Teresa in her work, and doctors and nurses also volunteered their services. Since 1952, many thousands of people from the Calcutta streets have been brought to *Nirmal Hriday*. About half of them have died in peace, and the others have survived.

Mother Teresa attends the dying at Nirmal Hriday.

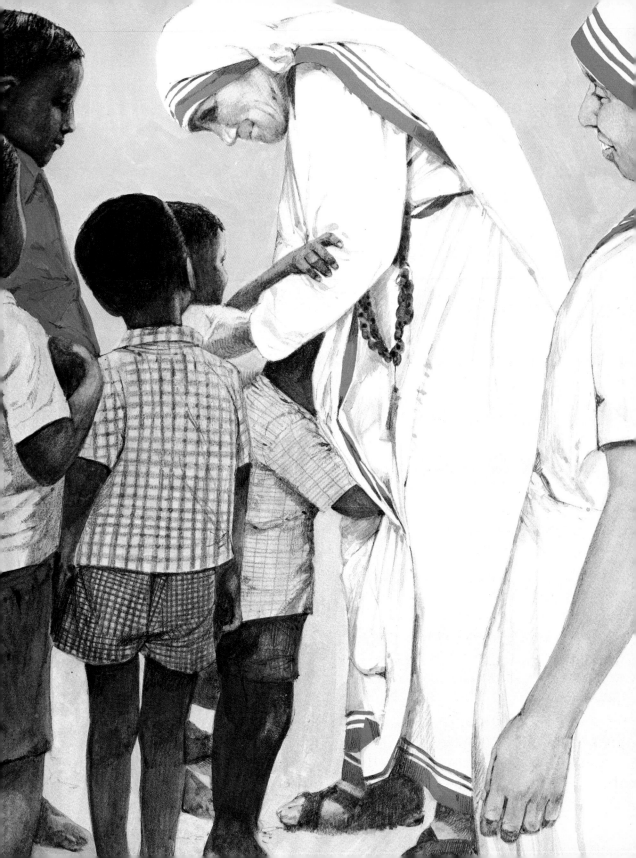

"Suffer little children"

Mother Teresa has a special place in her heart for the babies and little children often found abandoned in Calcutta's streets. Perhaps they have been left because their parents cannot afford to feed them, or simply do not want them. But, according to Mother Teresa, there are never too many children in the world. God, she says, ". . . provides for the flowers and the birds, for everything in the world that He has created. And those little children are His life. There can never be enough."

No child has ever been turned away from *Shishu Bhavan*, Mother Teresa's home for abandoned or dying children.

Most of the children arrive in terrible condition, covered with sores and lice, and sometimes suffering from tuberculosis. Some are orphans, others are crippled or mentally retarded. Yet they all have one thing in common, their need for love, which they get at *Shishu Bhavan*.

Sadly, many of the very small abandoned babies, some found in garbage cans and on refuse heaps, do not survive. But they are given every chance at the home. Lying in their little cots, the smallest ones, who are too tiny and weak to suck, are fed through their veins.

But the outlook for most of the children – so many of whom would have died without Mother Teresa and her helpers – is good. Some eventually go back to their families as happy, healthy youngsters. Others are adopted, sometimes going to live abroad. A few children stay with Mother Teresa, who sees that they are properly educated and may one day make happy marriages.

A Sister of Charity feeding babies.

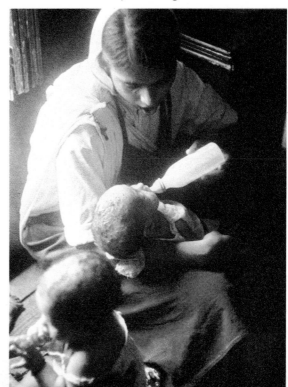

The outcasts

The terrible disease, leprosy, was mentioned in the Bible, and it is still a scourge today in countries where people are too poor to afford adequate food or shelter. It is a very infectious disease, causing sores on the skin and it can result in paralysis and deformity. In Calcutta alone, there are an estimated fifty thousand lepers. Some are well educated or rich, yet once they are afflicted with the disease, all lepers, rich or poor, become outcasts. They are abandoned by their families and friends and are reduced to begging.

In 1957, five lepers came to Mother Teresa for help. They had lost their jobs and could find nowhere to live. Mother Teresa established a shelter for them on the outskirts of the city, and soon a hundred and fifty were living there. Unfortunately, the shelter had to be demolished as the area was to be redeveloped.

But Mother Teresa was determined that, despite all the obstacles, the work for lepers would continue. There were possibly three million lepers in India, only a very few of whom

would be able to receive hospital care. She set up small dispensaries where lepers could obtain a new drug. Then the first mobile clinic was set up, run by a doctor and Missionaries of Charity specially trained in the treatment of leprosy.

A permanent leper clinic was opened on some land which Mother Teresa was offered in an industrial suburb of Calcutta. Today, this center, at Titigarh, has treated thousands of lepers as outpatients and many, in an advanced stage of the disease, as inmates. As well as being treated for their disease, the lepers are

A leper woman with her child, who does not have the disease.

taught skills such as carpentry and basketmaking.

Also on the site, 140 kilometers (86 miles) from Calcutta, Mother Teresa has founded the leper village of *Shanti Nagar*, which means Place of Peace. Here, leper families can live and learn new trades and can become almost selfsupporting.

21

"God will provide"

Receiving Holy Communion from Pope John Paul II.

"God will provide," is Mother Teresa's answer to all those who ask where the money will come from to fund a project. Her philosophy is very simple. She believes that God has put sufficient in the world for everyone – it's just a matter of sharing it.

Sometimes it has seemed like a miracle when desperately needed money has arrived in the nick of time. Once, she was told that a children's home was needed in an Indian town. It would cost 50,000 rupees, but Mother Teresa had no money. Then came the news that she had been given a special award from the Philippines – worth about 50,000 rupees!

When she wanted to open a convent in London, she was offered a large house for £6,000 ($8,400). Again Mother Teresa had no money, but during a tour of Britain, £5,995 was given to her by well-wishers.

In 1964, Pope Paul VI visited India and gave Mother Teresa the splendid car he had used during his visit. Instead of using it herself or simply selling it, Mother Teresa asked her helpers (called "Co-Workers") to raffle the car. They raised half a million rupees, and this money was used to establish a leper village.

With Co-Workers in England.

Opposition

Despite the value of Mother Teresa's work, she and her followers faced hostility in the early days. When the home for the dying was opened, threats were made and stones thrown by local people who complained that this "foreign lady" was getting the poor to change their religion, from Hinduism to Christianity.

One day, after receiving complaints, the Police Commissioner visited *Nirmal Hriday*. He saw Mother Teresa attending a sick patient covered with sores; the smell was terrible. He turned to those who had complained and agreed that he had said he would "push Mother Teresa out." "But before I do, you must get your mothers and sisters to do the work she is doing. Only then will I exercise my authority."

The trouble finally ended after Mother Teresa nursed a priest in the Kali Temple. He was dying of cholera. Then the people realized that she cares equally for all, whatever their religion.

A typical day

Mother Teresa and her Missionaries of Charity have always shared the same sort of existence as the poor people they serve. The nuns' lives seem particularly hard when we remember that many of them come from well-to-do backgrounds. Their possessions are simple and few – two white saris bordered with blue like the one Mother Teresa wears, a shining bucket in which to wash and their devotional books.

The Sisters' day begins at 4:30 a.m. with prayers and meditation, followed by Mass. When Mass is over, they do their washing and other domestic tasks. After a frugal breakfast, the nuns leave for their day's work at around 8 a.m. Mother Teresa is as tireless as her workers, leaving with them in the morning and often returning in the early evening without having had even a drink of water.

Their duties are many and varied. Some will go to the Home for the Dying, some to schools and dispensaries, some to look after the insane. Others will go to

care for the lepers or the many unwanted babies and children who come into their charge. They will bring practical and medical help, and also the gift of love, making even the most wretched feel cherished.

The Missionary Brothers of Charity – whose work began in 1963 – have the same frugal lifestyle as the Sisters. They started because Mother Teresa felt that there was a need for men to take care of the boys at school and the men in the Home for the Dying.

Once, Mother Teresa was asked whether it was a lot to expect of her followers to live like the poor and give all their time and energy to serving them. She replied: "That is what they want to give. They want to give to God everything. They know very well that it's to Christ the hungry and Christ the naked and Christ the homeless that they are doing it." And, she went on to explain: "They are not forced to be happy; they are naturally happy because they have found what they have looked for."

All over the world

"My people," is how Mother Teresa refers to the poor of the world, and since her work started in the slums of Calcutta, it has spread to all corners of that world. The Missionaries of Charity have provided homes for abandoned babies and for the dying; also clinics, training centers, schools, nurseries, leprosy care and mobile dispensaries. Then there are the millions of starving people who have been, and are being, cared for and fed every day.

For the first ten years, Mother Teresa and the Missionaries of Charity were busy working, and training more Sisters, in Calcutta. Their work became increasingly well known

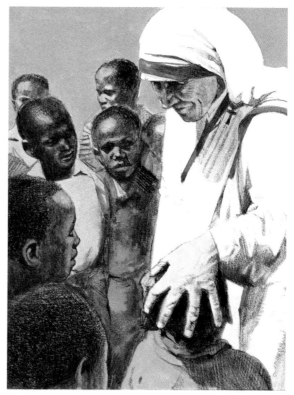

With children in Kenya.

Mother Teresa receives the Jewel of India, her adopted country's highest award.

throughout India and in 1960 they opened a children's home in Delhi. In Bombay, Mother Teresa opened a Home for the Destitute Dying after hearing of a woman dying in a busy street and lying there for many hours. Gradually a network of loving care grew throughout the whole country.

But Mother Teresa's work and compassion was needed outside India as well. In 1965, the Sisters and Brothers were given permission to work wherever they might be invited. That same year they went to Venezuela to feed the hungry and care for the old and the sick. That was only the beginning; today Missionaries of Charity are to be found on all the continents, the Americas, the Middle East, Australia, Africa, Asia and Europe.

Together, with the Co-Workers (helpers), the Brothers and Sisters have worked in the slums of Rome with Sicilian immigrants, helped Aborigines in Australia, cared for Arabs living in Israeli-occupied territory, and offered shelter, food and comfort to the destitute in London. Speaking of old people in Britain found dying, or dead, alone in their homes, Mother Teresa once said: "In England, they suffer from loneliness. They have no need for bread but they need human love. This is the hungry Christ for us."

On a visit to Ethiopia Mother Teresa talks to rock musician Bob Geldof, who organized the raising of funds for the famine-stricken people.

The world's thanks

Mother Teresa in Hong Kong, where she has opened a home for destitutes.

Over the years, Mother Teresa's work has been recognized by a grateful world. She has received many awards, including Pope John XXIII's Peace Prize, the John F. Kennedy International Award, the Jawaharlal Nehru Award (presented by the Indian government) and the Templeton Award for Progress in Religion. She was the first person ever to receive this award, being chosen from over 2,000 nominees, and it was presented to her by the Duke of Edinburgh in 1973.

Yet the best known of all the honors she has received was the Nobel Peace Prize, which she accepted in the Norwegian capital, Oslo, in December, 1979. When told about winning the award she said: "Personally I am unworthy. I accept in the name of the poor, because I believe that by giving me the prize they have recognized the presence of the poor in the world." Although it was bitterly cold, she arrived in Oslo still wearing her thin sari and carrying a shopping bag. Even before the actual presentation ceremony, the people of Norway were anxious to show the tiny nun how much they loved her. Schoolchildren handed her a 175 dollars check, and a

She receives funds from well-wishers all over the world.

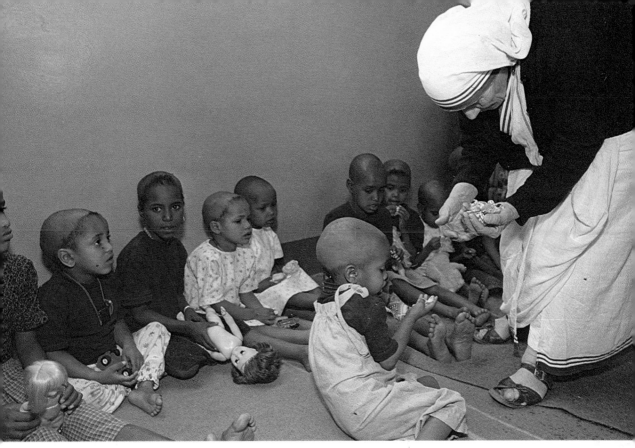

Mother Teresa in Ethiopia with children rescued from the famine.

further 70,000 dollars was collected by young people all over the country.

Mother Teresa received the Nobel Peace Prize from the King of Norway and a check for 190,000 dollars was given to her. The prize money would go, she said, to feed the poor and build more homes for the homeless and people suffering from leprosy. And, very typically, she asked that the money which would have been spent on a celebration banquet in Oslo be spent, instead, on the poor and the lepers in India. This money, she explained, was sufficient to buy meals in Calcutta for 15,000 people.

Morarji Desai, Prime Minister of India at that time, summed up the feelings of people everywhere when they learned that the great honor of the Nobel Peace Prize had been awarded to Mother Teresa. "Many great people have trod this earth, but very few of these have been good people. Mother Teresa is good as well as great," he said.

Important dates

1910 (August 27) Birth of Agnes Gouxha Bejaxhiu.

1928 She is sent to Loreto Abbey, near Dublin, and from there to Darjeeling in India, to begin her period as a novice. Takes the name of Sister Teresa.

1928–1948 Teaches at St Mary's High School in Calcutta. Later becomes principal of the school.

1931 Takes her first vows in Darjeeling.

1937 Takes her final vows in Loreto School, Darjeeling.

1946 (September 10) Inspiration Day.

1948 (August) Wearing a white, blue-bordered sari, Mother Teresa leaves the convent to begin her work outside.
She opens her first slum school in Calcutta and becomes an Indian citizen.

1950 The new Congregation of the Missionaries of Charity is approved by the Pope and is instituted in Calcutta. From there the Congregation spreads all over India.

1952 Home for the Destitute Dying (*Nirmal Hriday*) opened.

1953 Home for abandoned and dying children (*Shishu Bhavan*) opened.

1957 Leper village (*Shanti Nagar*) founded.

1963 Missionary Brothers of Charity formed.

1965 Work of the Missionaries of Charity begins outside India, in Venezuela, and from there spreads all over the world.

1979 Mother Teresa receives the Nobel Peace Prize.

1982 (August) She goes as special envoy for Pope John Paul II to war-torn Beirut in Lebanon.

1985 (January) She visits famine-stricken Ethiopia.

Books to read

Craig, Mary. *Mother Teresa*. North Pomfret, VT: David & Charles, 1983.

Green, Carol. *Mother Teresa: Friend of the Friendless*. Chicago, IL: Childrens Press, 1983.

Lee, Betsy. *Mother Teresa: Caring for All God's Children*. Minneapolis, MN: Dillon Press, 1981.

Sebba, Anne. *Mother Teresa*. New York: Franklin Watts, 1982.

Glossary

Buddhist   A follower of Buddhism, a religion springing from the philosophical teachings of Gautama Buddha, the son of an Indian nobleman, living in the sixth century B.C.

Congregation of the Missionaries of Charity   The Society founded by Mother Teresa. The Congregation members follow Mother Teresa's way of life and are bound by simple religious vows.

Destitute   Without money, food or shelter.

Dispensary   A clinic where medicines can be obtained.

Hindu   Someone who practices Hinduism, the religion of the majority of Indian people. Hinduism is based on one god, who takes many forms.

Leprosy   A chronic infectious disease occuring mainly in tropical countries. Untreated, it can cause painful swellings of the skin, disfigurement and deformities.

Missionary   Someone who undertakes to spread the Christian religion to nonbelievers.

Muslim   A believer in the religion of Islam, which teaches submission to one God (Allah) and living according to the words of the Prophet Muhammad.

Nobel Prizes   Awards made every year for achievements in science, economics, literature and peace. They are considered to be the world's highest honor.

Novice   A person who is received on probation into a religious order, before taking vows.

Nun   A woman belonging to a religious order.

Patriot   Someone who loves their native country and supports it in every way possible.

Take vows   Make promises, when entering a religious order, to obey the rules of poverty, chastity and obedience.

Picture credits

Index